mushrooms

mushrooms

Great recipe ideas with a classic ingredient

›› in 60 ways

The publisher wishes to thank Sia Huat Pte Ltd for the loan and use of their tableware.

Design: Sri Putri Julio
Photography: Jambu Studio

Copyright © 2006 Marshall Cavendish International (Asia) Private Limited

Published by Marshall Cavendish Cuisine
An imprint of Marshall Cavendish International
1 New Industrial Road, Singapore 536196

All rights reserved

No part of this publication may be reproduced, stored in a retrieval system or transmitted, in any form or by any means, electronic, mechanical, photocopying, recording or otherwise, without the prior permission of the copyright owner. Request for permission should be addressed to the Publisher, Marshall Cavendish International (Asia) Private Limited, 1 New Industrial Road, Singapore 536196. Tel: (65) 6213 9300, Fax: (65) 6285 4871. E-mail: te@sg.marshallcavendish.com

Limits of Liability/Disclaimer of Warranty: The Author and Publisher of this book have used their best efforts in preparing this book. The Publisher makes no representation or warranties with respect to the contents of this book and is not responsible for the outcome of any recipe in this book. While the Publisher has reviewed each recipe carefully, the reader may not always achieve the results desired due to variations in ingredients, cooking temperatures and individual cooking abilities. The Publisher shall in no event be liable for any loss of profit or any other commercial damage, including but not limited to special, incidental, consequential, or other damages.

Other Marshall Cavendish Offices:
Marshall Cavendish Ltd. 119 Wardour Street, London W1F 0UW, UK • Marshall Cavendish Corporation. 99 White Plains Road, Tarrytown NY 10591-9001, USA • Marshall Cavendish International (Thailand) Co Ltd. 253 Asoke, 12th Flr, Sukhumvit 21 Road, Klongtoey Nua, Wattana, Bangkok 10110, Thailand • Marshall Cavendish (Malaysia) Sdn Bhd, Times Subang, Lot 46, Subang Hi-Tech Industrial Park, Batu Tiga, 40000 Shah Alam, Selangor Darul Ehsan, Malaysia

Marshall Cavendish is a trademark of Times Publishing Limited

National Library Board Singapore Cataloguing in Publication Data

Mushrooms in 60 ways. – Singapore : Marshall Cavendish Cuisine, c2006.
p. cm. – (In 60 ways)
ISBN-13 : 978-981-261-247-2
ISBN-10 : 981-261-247-5

1. Cookery (Mushrooms) I. Title: Mushrooms in sixty ways
II. Series: In 60 ways

TX804
641.658 -- dc21   SLS2006007234

Printed in Singapore by Times Graphics Pte Ltd

contents

introduction **7**
soups **9**
snacks & appetisers **27**
meat & poultry **57**
vegetables & salads **83**
seafood **107**
rice & noodles **123**
glossary **140**
weights & measures **144**

introduction >>

Since ancient history, mushrooms have been a prized food item. The Egyptian Pharaohs believed that it was the plant of immortality, while the Romans viewed mushrooms as food from the gods. The Greeks ate mushrooms for a source of strength and the Chinese prize them for their medicinal and healing properties. Previously gathered from the wilderness by women, mushrooms today are predominantly cultivated, making numerous varieties such as the shiitake and enokitake mushrooms that are native to parts of Asia widely available worldwide.

Low in salt and fat content but high in potassium, riboflavin, niacin, and selenium, mushrooms are low in calories and are highly nutritious. Mushrooms are also a good source of fibre. When preparing and cleaning mushrooms, never soak fresh mushrooms. Instead, use a damp cloth to wipe mushroom caps and a brush to brush off dirt. To remove stems, gently twist off or gently push the stems from side to side until they come loose.

When choosing mushrooms, check that they are firm and meaty, and ensure that the gills under the mushroom are light-coloured. Fresh mushrooms should smell earthy. Discard mushrooms if they are slimy, bruised or discoloured.

Water constitutes 80–90 per cent of mushrooms, hence these delicate fungi can deteriorate quickly if not stored appropriately. To prevent the loss of moisture and rapid deterioration, mushrooms should be wrapped with absorbent paper or stored in paper bags in the lowest section of the refrigerator.

Mushrooms are valued in the kitchen for their texture and earthy flavours. Their porous nature enables them to take on flavours and at the same time impart their own to a dish. When using dried mushrooms, strain and use the liquid that was used to soak the mushrooms as a stock for cooking. With over 3,000 edible varieties, mushrooms offer different textures and tastes to tease the taste buds. The mushroom varieties used in this book—shiitake, wood ear, oyster, portobello, straw, white button, honshimeiji, enokitake and swiss brown—are by no means exhaustive, but are commonly found and available in most fresh food markets and supermarkets today.

soups

mint and mushroom soup **10**
consommé aux champignons **13**
cream of mushroom soup **14**
tom yum mushroom soup **17**
balinese mushroom soup **18**
miso soup with honshimeiji mushrooms **21**
three-mushroom and chicken soup **22**
straw mushroom and egg soup **25**

mint and mushroom soup

A smooth and delicately flavoured soup, Mint and Mushroom Soup makes a delightful first course for a dinner party. Alternatively, serve with crusty bread, butter and a salad, as a very simple light lunch.

Serves 4

Ingredients

Potatoes	4, large, peeled and coarsely chopped
Onion	1, peeled and coarsely chopped
Chicken stock	750 ml (24 fl oz / 3 cups)
Lemon	1, squeezed for juice and grated for zest
Chopped fresh rosemary	1 Tbsp
Salt	1 tsp
Ground black pepper	½ tsp
Butter	125 g (4 ½ oz)
White button mushrooms	250 g (8 oz), wiped clean and sliced
Plain (all-purpose) flour	1 Tbsp
Finely chopped fresh mint leaves	2 Tbsp
Double (heavy) cream	150 ml (5 fl oz / ⅝ cup)

Method

- Place potatoes and onion in a large saucepan. Pour in stock, lemon zest and juice, rosemary, salt and pepper. Place pan over high heat and bring mixture to the boil. Reduce heat to low and simmer, stirring occasionally for 25 minutes, or until vegetables are tender.

- Meanwhile, in a small saucepan, melt butter over low heat. Add mushrooms and toss in butter until thoroughly coated. Cook slowly, stirring occasionally for 10 minutes. With a wooden spoon, stir flour into mushroom mixture. Remove from heat and set aside.

- With a slotted spoon, remove potatoes and onion from stock mixture. Purée in food mill, or rub through a strainer using the back of a wooden spoon. Return puréed vegetable to stock mixture.

- Add mushrooms to stock mixture. Increase heat to high and bring soup to the boil, stirring constantly. Stir in mint leaves and 125 ml (4 fl oz / ½ cup) cream Remove pan from heat.

- Ladle soup into individual soup bowls. Add 1 tsp of cream to each bowl. Garnish as desired and serve immediately.

consommé aux champignons

Consommé aux Champignons is a simple variation of the basic consommé, and is easy to make.

Serves 6

Ingredients

Beef bouillon	1.25 litres (40 fl oz / 5 cups)
White button mushrooms	350 g (12 oz), caps wiped and finely diced
Salt	1 tsp
Ground white pepper	½ tsp
Sherry	2 Tbsp

Method

- In a pot, bring bouillon to the boil over moderate heat.
- Add mushrooms, reduce heat to low, cover pan and simmer for 15–20 minutes or until mushrooms are tender.
- Stir in salt and pepper. Taste consommé and add more seasoning if necessary. Stir in sherry and serve immediately.

cream of mushroom soup

Always a popular soup, this dish is quick and easy to prepare. Serve it with buttered toast to make a nourishing appetiser or lunch.

Serves 4

Ingredients

Butter	50 g (2 oz)
White button mushrooms	220 g (8 oz), wiped and sliced
Spring onion (scallion)	1, finely chopped
Chicken stock	375 ml (12 fl oz / 1½ cups)
Milk	150 ml (5 fl oz / ⅝ cup)
Plain (all-purpose) flour	2 Tbsp
Single (light) cream	150 ml (5 fl oz / ⅝ cup)
Salt	½ tsp
Ground white pepper	½ tsp

Method

- In a medium-sized saucepan, melt 40 g (1¼ oz) butter over moderate heat. Add mushrooms and spring onion and sauté for 3 minutes.
- Add chicken stock and milk to pan then bring to the boil. Reduce heat to low, cover and simmer for 20 minutes.
- Put mixture in an electric blender (processor) or through a food mill and purée until smooth.
- In a large saucepan, melt remaining butter over moderate heat. Remove pan from heat and stir in flour, mixing to a smooth paste. Return pan to heat and gradually add blended soup, stirring continuously until it comes to the boil.
- Reduce heat and stir in cream, salt and pepper.
- Reheat soup without allowing it to boil again. Serve immediately.

tom yum mushroom soup

This refreshing spicy hot and sour soup will tingle your taste buds.
Serves 6–8

Ingredients

Water	750 ml (24 fl oz / 3 cups)
Oyster mushrooms	500 g (1 lb 1 oz), torn into three pieces each
Straw mushrooms	500 g (1 lb 1 oz), halved
Lemon grass	2 stalks, bruised
Kaffir lime leaves	2, roughly shredded
Coriander leaves (cilantro)	2 sprigs, chopped
Red bird's eye chillies	10, thinly sliced
Dried red chillies	2
Limes	3–4, squeezed for juice
Canned bamboo shoots	50 g (2 oz), sliced
Thai fish sauce	2–3 Tbsp

Chillies in oil (*nam prik pao*)

Peanut oil	4 Tbsp
Minced garlic	3 Tbsp
Minced shallots	3 Tbsp
Minced dried chillies	3 Tbsp
Prawn (shrimp) paste	1 Tbsp
Thai fish sauce	1 Tbsp
Sugar	to taste

Method

- Prepare chillies in oil. Heat oil in a sauce pan, add garlic and shallots and fry briefly. Remove from oil and set aside.
- In the same pan, add chillies and fry until they start to change colour, then remove and set aside.
- Using a mortar and pestle, pound prawn paste, chillies, fried garlic and shallots until well blended. Over low heat, return chilli paste mixture to pan. Add fish sauce and sugar to taste. Mix until a smooth paste is formed.
- Bring water to the boil, add chillies in oil and all ingredients. Keep stirring until mushrooms are cooked.
- Ladle soup into serving bowls and serve hot.

balinese mushroom soup

Served with steamed rice, this creamy and flavourful soup becomes a hearty meal.

Serves 4

Ingredients

Cooking oil	2 Tbsp
Shiitake mushrooms	250 g (9 oz), caps wiped and quartered
Chicken stock	625 ml (20 fl oz / 2½ cups)
Lemon grass	1 stalk, bruised
Kaffir lime leaves	2, shredded
Coconut cream	250 ml (8 fl oz / 1 cup)
Salt	a pinch
Ground black pepper	a pinch
Crisp-fried shallots (optional)	2 Tbsp

Spice Paste

Red chillies	125 g (4½ oz), halved, lengthways, seeded and sliced
Shallots	50 g (2 oz), peeled and sliced
Garlic	50 g (2 oz), peeled and sliced
Galangal	50 g (2 oz), peeled and chopped
Turmeric	50 g (2 oz), peeled and sliced
Candlenuts	100 g (4 oz), crushed
Coriander seeds	½ Tbsp, crushed
Black peppercorns	1 tsp, crushed
Cooking oil	60 ml (2 fl oz / ¼ cup)

Method

- Prepare spice paste. Using a mortar and pestle, pound all spice paste ingredients until a smooth paste is formed.
- Heat oil in a heavy saucepan. Add 2 Tbsp spice paste and sauté until fragrant. Add mushrooms and sauté for another 2 minutes.
- Add stock, lemon grass and lime leaves. Bring to the boil over low heat and simmer for another 5 minutes.
- Add coconut cream. Return to the boil and simmer for 5 minutes.
- Season with salt and pepper to taste. Garnish with crisp-fried shallots, if desired. Serve hot.

miso soup with honshimeiji mushrooms

This popular Japanese soup is often served as part of a Japanese meal.

Serves 4

Ingredients

Instant dashi	2 tsp
Water	1 litre (32 fl oz / 4 cups)
Soft bean curd	1 piece, 200 g (7 oz), cut into 1-cm ($1/2$-in) cubes
Honshimeiji mushrooms	200 g (7 oz)
Red miso paste	3–4 Tbsp
Spring onions (scallions)	2, chopped

Method

- In a deep pot, add dashi to water and bring to the boil.
- Add bean curd cubes and mushrooms, simmer gently for 3–5 minutes, or until mushrooms are cooked.
- Stir in miso paste until it dissolves completely. Remove from heat and ladle into bowls. Garnish with spring onions and serve hot.

Be careful not to overboil the soup as miso paste will lose its flavour.

three-mushroom and chicken soup

This soup, consisting of a trio of mushrooms and chicken, is comforting and nutritious.

Serves 4

Ingredients

Dried Chinese mushrooms	4, stems discarded
Hot water	250 ml (8 fl oz / 1 cup)
Chicken thighs	6, cut into 3 pieces each
Canned button mushrooms	10, halved
Straw mushrooms	5, halved
Carrot	1, small, diced
Light soy sauce	2 Tbsp
Sugar	½ tsp
Tomatoes	4, halved
Soft bean curd	1, cut into small squares
Coriander leaves (cilantro)	1 sprig

Method

- Soak dried Chinese mushrooms in hot water for 1 hour. Drain and squeeze out excess liquid from mushrooms. Reserve soaking liquid.
- In a small steaming pot, add soaking liquid and top up with boiling water to half-fill pot. Add chicken, mushrooms and diced carrot. Season with soy sauce and sugar.
- Position a steaming rack in a large metal pot. Set steaming pot on rack and fill larger pot with water until 2.5-cm (1-in) of smaller pot is submerged.
- Cover larger pot and steam for 30 minutes. Add tomatoes and soft bean curd to smaller pot. Steam for another 10 minutes.
- Garnish with coriander leaves and serve hot.

straw mushroom and egg soup

This egg drop soup is delicate in taste and visually pleasing.
Serves 4

Ingredients

Water	800 ml (26 fl oz / 3¼ cups)
Straw mushrooms	400 g (13½ oz), halved
Eggs	3
Salt	to taste
Coriander leaves (cilantro)	3 sprigs, cut into 2.5-cm (1-in) lengths
Spring onion (scallion)	1, finely chopped
Light soy sauce	½ Tbsp
Sesame oil	½ tsp
Ground white pepper	a dash

Method

- Bring water to the boil and add mushrooms.
- Whisk eggs lightly with salt and pour gradually in a long thin stream into mushroom soup, stirring constantly.
- Place coriander, spring onion, soy sauce and sesame oil into a big serving bowl. Pour hot soup over, season with pepper and serve immediately.

snacks & appetisers

shiitake tempura **28**

oriental stuffed mushrooms **31**

mushroom samosas **32**

baked stuffed mushrooms **35**

shiitake mushroom dumplings **36**

creamy mushrooms **39**

vegetarian mushroom spring rolls **40**

deep-fried mushrooms **43**

mushroom omelette with oyster sauce **44**

provençal-style mushrooms **47**

mushrooms with bean curd stuffing **48**

braised black mushrooms **51**

fried mushrooms with eggs on toast **52**

mini mushroom and cheese pies **55**

shiitake tempura

Always a crowd pleaser, these crispy battered shiitake mushrooms make perfect crunchy nibbles or are great as an appetiser.

Serves 4

Ingredients

Cooking oil	500 ml (16 fl oz / 2 cups)
Shiitake mushrooms	200 g (7 oz), caps wiped and stems discarded
Plain (all-purpose) flour (for dusting)	110 g (4 oz)

Tempura Batter

Egg yolk	1/2
Iced water	125 ml (4 fl oz / 1/2 cup)
Rice flour	110 g (4 oz)

Tempura Dipping Sauce

Light soy sauce	125 ml (4 fl oz / 1/2 cup)
Rice wine vinegar	125 ml (4 fl oz / 1/2 cup)
Sugar	2 Tbsp
Spring onions (scallions)	2, chopped
Ginger	2.5-cm (1-in) knob, peeled and grated

Method

- Prepare tempura batter. Lightly beat egg yolk in a mixing bowl and gently mix in iced water. Add rice flour and loosely combine with a fork. Batter should be slightly lumpy.
- In a another bowl, combine all ingredients for tempura dipping sauce. Mix well and set aside.
- Heat oil in a wok or deep-fryer to 200°C (400°F). Lightly dust mushrooms with flour, shaking off any excess. Dip into tempura batter and slowly lower into oil one by one.
- Fry for about 5–6 minutes turning over once. Fry until golden brown. Remove and drain on absorbent paper. Serve immediately with dipping sauce.

NOTE

Do not fry more than 6 mushrooms at a time as this will cause overcrowding and prevent the tempura from turning crispy and brown.

oriental stuffed mushrooms

These shiitake mushrooms stuffed with minced pork, water chestnuts and spring onions make tasty meaty bites.

Serves 8

Ingredients

Minced pork	175 g (6 oz)
Water chestnuts	50 g (2 oz), chopped
Spring onions (scallions)	4, sliced
Shiitake mushrooms	24, stems removed and minced, caps left whole
Ginger	1-cm ($1/2$-in) knob, peeled and grated
Chinese cooking wine (*hua tiao*)	2 tsp
Light soy sauce	1 tsp
Hoi sin sauce	$1/2$ tsp
Roasted white sesame seeds	1 Tbsp
Egg white	1
Ground white pepper	a dash
Dried breadcrumbs	2 Tbsp

Method

- Preheat oven to 200°C (400°F).
- Mix minced pork, water chestnuts, 3 spring onions and minced mushroom stems. Add ginger, wine, soy sauce, hoi sin sauce, sesame seeds and egg white. Season with pepper and leave to marinate for 10 minutes.
- Divide pork mixture into 24 equal portions. Spoon each portion into the cavities of mushroom caps, shaping them to form mounds.
- Sprinkle breadcrumbs over mushrooms. Place mushrooms on a greased baking tray and bake mushrooms in the middle of the oven for 7–10 minutes, or until filling is heated through.
- To make filling crisp, cooked mushrooms may be put under a preheated broiler about 10-cm (4-in) from heat for 1 minute. Garnish with remaining spring onion and serve immediately.

mushroom samosas

These Indian spiced mushroom samosas make great appetisers for parties as they are easy to prepare and can be made in advance.

Makes 10

Ingredients

Filo pastry	10 sheets, each 27.5 x 18.75-cm (11 x 7½-in)
Melted butter	4 Tbsp
Cooking oil for frying	

Filling

Potatoes	200 g (7 oz)
Peas	20 g (¾ oz)
Onion	1, peeled and minced
Green chillies	6, seeded and minced
Ground coriander	2 tsp
Garam masala	1 tsp
Salt	2 tsp
Black mustard seeds	1 tsp
White button mushrooms	100 g (3½ oz), caps wiped and sliced

Method

- Cover potatoes and peas with water in a pot and bring to the boil. Reduce heat and simmer until potatoes are cooked and tender. Drain well. Peel potatoes and mash peas and potatoes separately.

- Heat oil in a frying pan and sauté onion, green chillies, ground coriander, garam masala, salt and mustard seeds until fragrant. Add mushrooms, peas and potatoes and sauté until well mixed. Set aside to cool.

- Brush each filo pastry sheet with melted butter then fold in half lengthways. Place a portion of filling on the bottom right hand corner then fold pastry over to form a triangle. Continue to fold to the top of the sheet then moisten end to seal.

- Heat oil for deep-frying, gently lower samosas into oil and fry until golden and crisp. Drain well on absorbent paper. Serve immediately with sweet chilli sauce if desired.

baked stuffed mushrooms

These mushrooms, stuffed with bacon and onion then topped off with breadcrumbs, have a crunchy bite and a faint smoky flavour from the bacon and paprika.

Serves 6

Ingredients

Butter	2 Tbsp
Onion	½, peeled and finely chopped
Large white mushrooms	12, stems removed and chopped, caps wiped
Garlic	1 clove, peeled and finely chopped
Chopped fresh parsley	2 Tbsp
Bacon	3 slices, fried, drained and crumbled
Dried breadcrumbs	350 g (12 oz) or less
Paprika	to taste
Salt	to taste
Ground black pepper	to taste
Olive oil	2 Tbsp

Method

- Preheat oven to 200°C (400°F).
- Heat butter in a frying pan over medium heat. Add onion and sauté for 1 minute.
- Add chopped mushroom stems and cook for about 2 minutes or until soft. Add garlic and parsley. Toss mixture to mix and cook for another minute. Remove from heat.
- Mix in crumbled bacon and add breadcrumbs half a cup at a time to ensure that just enough breadcrumbs are added to keep mixture moist. Season to taste with paprika, salt and pepper.
- When mixture is cool enough to handle, divide into 12 equal portions. Press a portion each into underside of mushroom caps. Place stuffed caps in a baking dish and drizzle with olive oil.
- Bake for 12–15 minutes or until heated through and slightly browned. Transfer to a serving dish and serve immediately.

shiitake mushroom dumplings

These shiitake mushroom dumplings are a tasty variation of the popular siew mai dim sum dish.

Serves 4

Ingredients

Cooking oil	3 Tbsp
Ginger	1-cm ($1/2$-in) knob, peeled and grated
Garlic	2 cloves, peeled and minced
Spring onions (scallions)	3, minced
Shiitake mushrooms	120 g ($4^1/_2$ oz), stems discarded and minced
Minced pork	225 g ($7^1/_2$ oz)
Egg white	1
Wood ear fungus	30 g (1 oz), soaked to soften and minced
Chinese cooking wine (*hua tiao*)	4 Tbsp
Light soy sauce	2 Tbsp
Ground white pepper	a dash
Siew mai skin	16 sheets

Method

- Heat oil in a pan and sauté ginger, garlic and spring onions until fragrant and brown. Add minced shiitake mushrooms and cook until soft. Drain and set aside.

- Mix pork and egg white together. Add sautéed mushroom mixture, wood ear fungus and season with wine, soy sauce and pepper. Divide pork mixture into 16 portions.

- Spoon a portion of pork mixture onto a *siew mai* skin and bring the edges up to make an open top dumpling. Repeat to make 15 more dumplings. Arrange dumplings on a steaming plate.

- Cover and steam over rapidly boiling water for 10 minutes or until cooked. Serve with sweet chilli sauce if desired.

creamy mushrooms

A delicious dish of mushrooms, smothered in a creamy sauce spiced with paprika. It makes an excellent light snack or appetiser.

Serves 4

Ingredients

Butter	1 Tbsp + ½ tsp
White button mushrooms	220 g (8 oz), caps wiped and sliced
Salt	¼ tsp
Ground black pepper	½ tsp
Paprika	a pinch
Single (light) cream	90 ml (3 fl oz / 6 Tbsp)
Chopped fresh parsley	1 Tbsp

Method

- Melt 1 Tbsp butter in a small saucepan over moderate heat, until butter is foamy. When foam subsides, add mushrooms, salt and pepper to pan. Cook, stirring occasionally, for 4–5 minutes, or until mushrooms are cooked. Remove from heat.
- Stir paprika and cream into saucepan, mixing well with mushrooms and mushroom juices. Stir in parsley and serve immediately.

vegetarian mushroom spring rolls

These crisp spring rolls are filled with mushrooms of different textures. Prepare them ahead of time and simply deep-fry them just before serving.

Makes 12

Ingredients

Vietnamese rice paper	12 sheets, 20 cm (8 in) in diameter
Cooking oil	for frying

Filling

Dried Chinese mushrooms	3, soaked to soften, stems discarded and caps thinly sliced
Wood ear fungus	10 g ($1/3$ oz), soaked to soften and thinly shredded
Transparent (glass) noodles	20 g ($1/3$ oz), soaked to soften and cut into 5-cm (2-in) lengths
Firm bean curd	100 g ($3 1/2$ oz), pan-fried and thinly sliced
Shallots	2, peeled and minced
Carrot	1, small, finely shredded
Thai fish sauce	$2/3$ Tbsp
Garlic	1 clove, peeled and finely minced
Ground white pepper	a dash
Sugar	a pinch
Salt	a pinch
Egg	1, lightly beaten

Method

- Place all filling ingredients into a large bowl. Mix well and divide into 12 portions. Set aside.
- Brush rice paper with warm water to soften it. Place a portion of filling on the lower edge of rice paper then bring rice paper up to enclose filling. Fold left and right sides over then roll tightly into a cylinder. Set aside and cover with a damp towel. Repeat to make 11 more rolls.
- Heat oil in a wok for deep-frying. Deep-fry rolls until golden brown on all sides. Drain well on absorbent paper and serve immediately.

deep-fried mushrooms

Simply coating the button mushrooms with wholemeal breadcrumbs gives the mushrooms a crunchy bite.

Serves 6

Ingredients

Fresh tarragon	4 stalks, chopped
Fresh wholemeal breadcrumbs	100 g (3½ oz)
White button mushrooms	225 g (7½ oz), caps wiped and trimmed
Plain (all-purpose) flour	2 Tbsp
Eggs	2, beaten
Cooking oil for deep-frying	

Garlic Dip

Greek-style yoghurt	4 Tbsp
Mayonnaise	3 Tbsp
Garlic	2 cloves, peeled and mashed with 1 tsp salt
Tomato purée	1 Tbsp

Method

- Mix chopped tarragon with breadcrumbs and set aside. Dip each mushroom in flour, then in beaten egg and finally in breadcrumb mixture. Place coated mushrooms on a plate and refrigerate until ready to cook.

- Mix ingredients for dip together and set aside.

- Heat oil in a wok or deep-fryer. Divide mushrooms into 6 batches. Gently lower a batch into oil and deep-fry for 3 minutes or until crisp and golden brown. Drain well. Repeat with remaining batches.

- Serve immediately with prepared dip.

mushroom omelette with oyster sauce

Light and nutritious, this omelette is perfect as a snack.
Serves 2–4

Ingredients

Cooking oil	4 Tbsp
Garlic	2 cloves, peeled and crushed
Shiitake mushrooms	200 g (7oz), stems discarded and thinly sliced
Oyster mushrooms	200 g (7oz), torn
Enokitake mushrooms	200 g (7oz), trimmed, separated
Wood ear fungus	100 g (3 1/2 oz)
Finely chopped fresh basil	2 Tbsp
Finely chopped fresh garlic chives	2 Tbsp
Salt	to taste
Ground black pepper	to taste
Eggs	8
Light soy sauce	2 tsp
Oyster sauce	2 Tbsp

Method

- Heat 1 Tbsp oil in a wok over medium-high heat until smoking. Add garlic and shiitake mushrooms and stir-fry for 1 minute or until fragrant.
- Add oyster mushrooms and stir-fry for 1 minute or until tender. Remove from heat.
- Add enokitake, wood ear fungus, basil and chives, and gently toss to combine, allowing the residual heat in the pan to cook the mixture. Taste and season with salt and pepper. Transfer to a large bowl and cover with foil to keep warm. Set aside.
- Crack eggs into a medium-sized bowl. Add soy sauce and whisk with fork until combined.
- Heat 1 Tbsp oil in a medium-sized frying pan over medium-high heat. Pour in half the egg mixture and tilt pan slightly so mixture covers the base of pan evenly. As omelette sets, gently lift edge so any uncooked egg runs underneath. Cook for 2 minutes or until just set. Slide omelette onto a large plate and cover with foil to keep warm. Repeat to make another omelette.
- Divide mushroom mixture among omelettes. Fold omelette in half to enclose filling. Drizzle with oyster sauce, garnish as desired and serve immediately.

provençal-style mushrooms

A classy way of cooking mushrooms; these mushrooms are flavoured with garlic and a hint of herbs. A great vegetable accompaniment to almost any meat or fish dish.

Serves 6

Ingredients

White button mushrooms	900 g (2 lb), caps wiped, stems removed and chopped
Dry white wine	125 ml (4 fl oz / ½ cup)
Butter	2 Tbsp
Onion	1, peeled and finely chopped
Garlic	2 cloves, peeled and crushed
Salt	½ tsp
Ground black pepper	½ tsp
Chopped fresh parsley	1 Tbsp
Dried thyme	½ tsp
Lemons	2, squeezed for juice

Method

- Place mushroom caps in a large saucepan and pour in wine. Set pan over moderately high heat and bring to the boil. Reduce heat to low and simmer mushrooms gently for 8 minutes. Remove pan from heat. Using a slotted spoon, transfer mushrooms to a plate and set aside. Discard pan liquid.

- Melt butter in a large frying pan over moderate heat until it foams. When foam subsides, add onion and garlic and sauté for 5–7 minutes or until onion is soft and translucent but not brown.

- Add mushroom caps, salt and pepper and sauté for 3 minutes. Finally, add mushroom stalks, parsley and thyme. Cook for another 2 minutes. Remove pan from heat.

- Transfer mushroom mixture into a warmed serving dish, drizzle with lemon juice and serve immediately.

mushrooms with bean curd stuffing

As an alternative to meat, bean curd is a good protein substitute. These mushroom stuffed with bean curd make elegant-looking appetisers for vegetarians.

Serves 4

Ingredients

Swiss brown mushrooms	6–8 (hollowed out), saving stems
Spring onions (scallions)	2, chopped
Garlic	2 cloves, peeled and crushed
Oyster sauce	1 Tbsp
Firm bean curd	1 piece, about 375 g (12½ oz), cut into 0.5-cm (¼-in) cubes
Corn kernels	200 g (7 oz)
Salt	to taste
Ground black pepper	to taste
Sesame oil	2 tsp

Method

- Preheat oven to 200°C (400°F).
- Chop mushroom stems and mix with spring onions, garlic and oyster sauce.
- Add bean curd and corn kernels to mushroom stem mixture. Season with salt and pepper. Mix well.
- Stuff mushrooms with bean curd mixture, and brush edges of mushrooms with sesame oil.
- Bake in oven for 12–15 minutes. Remove and serve immediately.

braised black mushrooms

A "must-have" at Chinese festive gatherings, because the mushroom cap symbolises an umbrella sheltering the family and holding it together.

Serves 4

Ingredients

Dried Chinese mushrooms	16, large
Hot water	750 ml (24 fl oz / 3 cups)
Cooking oil	2 Tbsp
Garlic	4 cloves, peeled and minced
Ginger	2-cm (1-in) knob, peeled, sliced and minced
Light soy sauce	1½ Tbsp
Dark soy sauce	1 Tbsp
Sesame oil	½ tsp

Method

- Soak mushrooms in hot water for 10–15 minutes. Drain, discard mushroom stems and squeeze out excess liquid from mushrooms. Reserve soaking liquid.
- Heat oil in a casserole and gently fry garlic and ginger until golden. Add drained mushrooms; stir-fry for a few minutes.
- Add soaking liquid and both soy sauces. Cover casserole tightly and simmer over very low heat for 2 hours. Check occasionally to make sure liquid does not dry out. Adding small amounts of water if necessary.
- Remove and drizzle with sesame oil just before serving.

SNACKS & APPETISERS

fried mushrooms with eggs on toast

Fantastic for a lazy weekend brunch or breakfast, fried mushrooms with eggs, is a perfect meal that can be prepared without much work.

Serves 4

Ingredients

Olive oil	125 ml (4 fl oz / ½ cup)
Onion	1, peeled and finely chopped
Garlic	3 cloves, peeled and crushed
Ground turmeric	½ tsp
Salt	to taste
White button mushrooms	400 g (14 oz), caps wiped and diced
Ripe tomatoes	300 g (10½ oz), diced
Ground black pepper	to taste
Chopped fresh parsley	100 g (3½ oz)
Eggs	4
Hot buttered toast	4

Method

- Heat oil in a medium-sized frying pan over medium heat. Add onion, stirring occasionally, for 8 minutes or until light golden brown.
- Stir in garlic and turmeric. Season with salt to taste. Cook for another 2 minutes.
- Add mushrooms and tomatoes to frying pan. Cook, stirring, for 10 minutes or until most of the liquid has evaporated. Stir in parsley. Season with salt and pepper.
- Spread mixture out to cover pan base. Reduce heat to medium-low. Break eggs into mixture and cook, stirring constantly to scamble egg mixture in the pan. Cover to cook for another 5 minutes.
- Place toast on serving plates. Top with egg mixture. Season with salt and pepper to taste if desired. Serve immediately.

mini mushroom and cheese pies

These pastries make a good hors d'oeuvre served with party cocktails.
Makes 24

Ingredients

Butter	25 g (1 oz)
Cream cheese with herbs and garlic	75 g (2½ oz)
Dill weed	½ tsp
White button mushrooms	100 g (3½ oz), caps wiped and finely chopped
Salt	to taste
Ground black pepper	to taste
Frozen shortcrust pastry	350 g (12 oz), defrosted
Egg yolk for glazing	1, lightly beaten

Method

- Preheat oven to 180°C (350°F). Grease baking tray with butter.
- In a clean, dry bowl, mash cream cheese and dill weed together until combined. Stir in mushrooms. Season to taste with salt and pepper then refrigerate.
- Meanwhile, roll out pastry to 0.5-cm (¼-in) thickness on a lightly floured work surface. Using a round pastry cutter or the rim of a glass, cut out 24 circles about 9-cm (3½ -in) in diameter.
- Place 1 tsp mushroom and cheese mixture onto one half of each circle, taking care not to overfill pastry circles or they will be very difficult to seal. Fold into half-moon shapes, wet edges with water and press firmly down to seal. Repeat until all filling is used.
- Arrange pies on a greased baking tray and glaze each one with a little egg yolk. Bake in oven for 30–40 minutes until pastry is cooked and golden in colour. Transfer to a warmed serving plate and serve at once.

meat & poultry

claypot beef, mushrooms and spring onions **58**

steamed mushrooms and chicken wings **61**

creamy mushroom chicken **62**

bacon, cheese and mushroom scones **65**

chicken and mushroom pie **66**

almond and chicken with mushrooms **69**

mushroom and beef stroganoff **70**

enokitake mushrooms wrapped in bacon **73**

chicken and mushroom croquettes **74**

macaroni with cheese and mushrooms **77**

five-spice pork, mushroom and almond stir-fry **78**

chinese chicken and mushroom parcels **81**

claypot beef, mushrooms and spring onions

This quick one-pot dish consisting of beef, mushrooms and spring onions is delightful with rice.

Serves 4

Ingredients

Fillet steak	500 g (1 lb 1½ oz)
Light soy sauce	1 Tbsp
Dark soy sauce	2 tsp
Ground black pepper	1 tsp
Sesame oil	½ tsp
Oyster sauce	2 Tbsp
Sugar	1 tsp
Corn flour (cornstarch)	1 Tbsp
Chinese rice wine (*hua tiao*)	1 Tbsp
Cooking oil	2 Tbsp
Garlic	2 cloves, peeled and chopped
Ginger	10 thin slices
Carrot	1, cut into thin rounds
Canned button mushrooms	15, halved
Water	3 Tbsp
Spring onions (scallions)	10 stalks, cut into 2.5-cm (1-in) lengths

Method

- Cut steak into 1-cm (½-in) thick slices then cut each slice into 3 pieces. Marinate in light and dark soy sauce, pepper, sesame oil, oyster sauce, sugar, corn flour and rice wine for 15 minutes.
- Heat oil in claypot and brown garlic. Add sliced ginger and carrot and fry for 2 minutes.
- Add mushrooms and stir-fry for another 2 minutes.
- Add steak pieces and water. Cook for 2 more minutes then add spring onions. Cover and cook for another minute.
- Add light soy sauce to taste. Serve hot.

steamed mushrooms and chicken wings

The chicken essence released during the cooking process infuses with the mushroom stock, making it a wonderful dish to enjoy with a bowl of hot fragrant white rice.

Serves 4

Ingredients

Dried Chinese mushrooms	20, stems discarded
Boiling water	375 ml (12 fl oz / 1½ cups)
Chicken wings	450 g (1 lb)
Salt	½ tsp
Ground white pepper	⅓ tsp
Sesame oil	½ tsp
Chinese cooking wine (*hua tiao*)	2 Tbsp
Ginger	2-cm (1-in) knob, peeled and shredded

Method

- Soak mushrooms in boiling water until softened. Drain and squeeze excess liquid from mushrooms. Reserve soaking liquid.
- Season chicken wings with salt, pepper, sesame oil, wine and ginger.
- Fill a Chinese porcelain steaming pot with seasoned chicken wings and mushrooms. Add soaking liquid and sufficient boiling water to half-fill the pot.
- Place steaming pot in a steamer over medium heat for 1 hour. As pot will be very hot, use oven gloves to remove it and place it on a large plate for easy handling when serving. Serve hot.

creamy mushroom chicken

This dish makes a great family dinner. Serve the chicken with golden sautéed potatoes and lightly cooked broccoli or cauliflower.

Serves 4

Ingredients

Chicken	1, about 1.5 kg (3 lb 4 1/2 oz)
Cooking oil, for brushing	
Fresh tarragon (optional)	to garnish

Stuffing

Butter	25 g (1 oz)
Onion	1, small, peeled and finely chopped
White button mushrooms	100 g (4 oz), caps wiped and chopped
Fresh white breadcrumbs	100 g (4 oz)
Lemon	1/2, squeezed for juice and grated for zest
Chopped fresh tarragon (optional)	2 tsp
Salt	to taste
Ground black pepper	to taste
Egg	1, lightly beaten

Mushroom Sauce

Plain (all-purpose) flour	3 Tbsp
Chicken stock	150 ml (5 fl oz)
Milk	300 ml (10 fl oz / 1 1/4 cups)
White button mushrooms	250 g (9 oz), caps wiped and finely sliced

Method

- Preheat oven to 190 °C (370°F).
- Prepare stuffing. Melt butter in a small saucepan, add onion and fry gently for 5 minutes or until soft and lightly coloured. Add mushrooms and cook for another 2 minutes. Set aside.
- In a large bowl, mix breadcrumbs, lemon zest and juice. Add tarragon, if using, and season lightly with salt and pepper. Mix in onion and mushroom mixture then stir in egg to bind. Set aside.
- Wash chicken and pat dry with absorbent paper. Spoon stuffing into neck cavity then fold skin back into position. Fold wing tips over neck and secure with a metal skewer.

- Place chicken in a roasting tin and brush with oil. Roast in the oven for 1 hour 30 minutes to 1 hour 45 minutes, basting occasionally, until chicken is tender and juices run clear when thickest part of thigh is pierced with metal skewer. Remove chicken and place on a heatproof (flameproof) serving dish. Reserve juices from roasting tin.
- Lower oven temperature to 110°C (225°F). Return chicken to oven to keep warm while preparing sauce.
- To prepare mushroom sauce, drain off fat from juices in roasting tin then place tin on the hob. Sprinkle in flour and stir, scraping all sediment from base and sides of tin. Cook over gentle heat for 1–2 minutes.
- Gradually stir in chicken stock then milk and slowly bring to the boil. Stir constantly until thickened and smooth then add sliced mushrooms and simmer for 5 minutes. Season to taste with salt and pepper.
- To serve, cut chicken into portions and drizzle a little sauce over. Pour remaining sauce into a warmed sauceboat and serve together with roast chicken.

bacon, cheese and mushroom scones

These savoury scones are perfect for breakfast or afternoon tea.
Serves 4

Ingredients

Butter	1 Tbsp
Bacon	200 g (7 oz), chopped
White button mushrooms	200 g (7 oz), caps wiped and chopped
Milk	250 ml (4 fl oz / 1 cup)
Melted butter	3 Tbsp
Egg	1
Salt	½ tsp
Grated Cheddar cheese	200 g (7 oz)
Baking powder	½ Tbsp
Plain (all-purpose) flour	200 g (7 oz / 2 cups)

Method

- Preheat oven to 200°C (400°F).
- Lightly grease muffin tins.
- Heat butter in a small saucepan and fry bacon until crispy. Remove and drain on absorbent paper. Set aside.
- Fry mushrooms in bacon fat left in pan, until well browned. Remove and drain on absorbent paper. Set aside.
- Mix milk, butter, egg and salt in large mixing bowl. Add cheese, bacon and mushrooms. Stir in baking powder and flour, until just mixed.
- Fill muffin tins until two-thirds full and bake for 15–20 minutes until golden brown. Allow scones to cool for a few minutes on a wire rack and serve warm.

chicken and mushroom pie

This rustic homely pie, made with shortcrust pastry, encloses a creamy chicken and mushroom filling.

Serves 4

Ingredients

Pastry Crust

Plain (all-purpose) flour	500 g (17½ oz / 5 cups)
Salt	½ tsp
Chilled butter	150 g (5 oz)
Egg yolk	30 g (1 oz) + extra for glazing
Cooking oil	4 Tbsp
Water	180 ml (6 fl oz / ¾ cup)

Filling

Cooking oil	2 Tbsp
Chicken thigh	500 g (17½ oz), cut into small cubes
Onion	1, peeled and diced
Garlic	2 cloves, peeled and chopped
White button mushrooms	100 g (3½ oz), caps wiped and diced
Chicken stock	500 ml (16 fl oz / 2 cups)
Salt	to taste
Ground black pepper	to taste
Corn flour (cornstarch)	2 tsp, mixed with 2 Tbsp water

Method

- Prepare pastry crust. Sieve flour and salt into a mixing bowl. Rub in butter until mixture resembles breadcrumbs. Mix in egg yolk, oil and water. Knead to form a firm dough. Chill for at least 1 hour, preferably overnight before using.

- Heat oil in a deep saucepan and brown chicken for about 5 minutes. Remove from pan and drain well on absorbent paper.

- Using the same pan, sauté onion and garlic until onion is translucent. Add browned chicken, mushrooms and chicken stock. Bring to the boil and simmer for 10 minutes. Season with salt and pepper then thicken with corn flour mixture. Pour into a flat tray. Set aside to cool for 10 minutes before refrigerating for about 1 hour.

- Preheat oven to 200°C (400°F).

- Roll out half the pastry dough to 0.5-cm (¼-in) thickness. Press pastry firmly into sides of a pie tin. Spoon filling in. Roll out remaining pastry dough and cover pie. Trim off any excess dough and seal edges by pressing down firmly. Glaze with egg yolk.

- Bake for 12–15 minutes until pastry crust turns golden brown. Serve hot.

almond and chicken with mushrooms

This quick and easy stir-fry dish of chicken, sugar peas, mushrooms and almonds is ideal for a weekday family dinner, served with white rice.

Serves 4

Ingredients

Cooking oil	250 ml (8 fl oz / 1 cup)
Almonds	50 g (2 oz), halved
Chicken breast	500 g (17½ oz), cut into 2-cm (1-in) cubes
White wine	2 tsp
Egg white	½
Corn flour (cornstarch)	1 tsp
Salt	to taste
Ground white pepper	to taste
Sugar peas	100 g (4 oz)
Water chestnuts	2, sliced
Canned bamboo shoots	50 g (2 oz), thinly sliced
Canned button mushrooms	24, halved

Sauce

Corn flour (cornstarch)	1 tsp
Chinese cooking wine (*hua tiao*)	1 Tbsp
Oyster sauce	1 Tbsp
Salt	½ tsp
Sugar	½ tsp

Method

- Heat oil in a wok and fry almonds until golden. Drain and set aside. Leave 2 Tbsp oil in wok for cooking chicken.
- Season chicken with wine, egg white and corn flour. Add salt and pepper to taste.
- Prepare sauce. In a small bowl, add corn flour, wine, oyster sauce, salt and sugar. Mix well and set aside.
- Reheat oil in wok and stir-fry chicken until meat turns white. Add sugar peas, water chestnuts, bamboo shoots and mushrooms. Stir-fry for another 3 minutes.
- Add sauce and stir-fry for another minute until ingredients are well coated.
- Transfer to a serving dish and top with fried almonds. Serve hot with rice.

mushroom and beef stroganoff

Stroganoff is an original Russian recipe that was invented by a chef in Saint Petersburg at a culinary competition during the period of the Czars.

Serves 4

Ingredients

Butter	1 Tbsp
Garlic	2 cloves, peeled and chopped
Onion	1, peeled and thinly sliced
Beef tenderloin	200 g (7 oz), sliced into strips
White button mushrooms	800 g (1¾ lb), caps wiped and sliced
Plain (all-purpose) flour	1 Tbsp
White wine	125 ml (4 fl oz / ½ cup)
Sour cream	250 ml (8 fl oz / 1 cup)
Ground nutmeg	¼ tsp
Salt	to taste
Ground black pepper	to taste
Cooked linguine	300 g (10½ oz)

Method

- Melt butter in a large pan over medium-high heat. Add garlic and sauté for 30 seconds. Add onion and sauté for 2 minutes.
- Add beef and mushrooms and sauté for 3 minutes. Reduce heat to medium. Stir in flour and cook for another minute.
- Add white wine and cook until mixture thickens, stirring frequently, for about 3 minutes.
- Mix in sour cream then add nutmeg. Season to taste with salt and pepper.
- Add linguine to pan. Toss until linguine is well-coated with sauce. Serve hot.

enokitake mushrooms wrapped in bacon

This simple dish brings out the best of both ingredients used. The subtly flavoured enokitake mushrooms absorb the smoky flavour of the bacon, making these bundles delightful savoury treats.

Serves 2

Ingredients

Enokitake mushrooms	1 bundle, 200 g (7 oz) stems trimmed
Bacon	6 slices

Method

- Preheat oven to 180°C (350°F).
- Divide enokitake mushrooms into 6 equal portions.
- Place a portion of mushrooms on one end of a bacon slice and roll up tightly. Secure by pushing a toothpick through the centre. Repeat to make 6 bundles.
- Arrange bundles on a greased baking tray and grill for 7 minutes before turning bundles over. Grill for another 7 minutes until bundles turn golden brown. Remove and serve immediately.

chicken and mushroom croquette

These chicken-and-mushroom filled potato cutlets are a favourite with both children and adults alike.

Serves 6

Ingredients

Butter	4 Tbsp
Plain (all-purpose) flour	5 Tbsp
Salt	1 tsp
Ground black pepper	1/4 tsp
Milk	250 ml (8 fl oz / 1 cup)
Cooked chicken breast	500 g (17 1/2 oz) diced
Canned button mushrooms	1 can, drained and small diced
Dry white breadcrumbs	450 g (1 lb)
Egg	1, beaten and mixed with 1 Tbsp water

Method

- Melt butter in a saucepan. Stir in flour, salt and pepper. Continue stirring and gradually add milk. Cook, stirring over low heat until mixture is smooth and thick. Mix in chicken and mushrooms.
- Spread mixture out on a medium-sized pan. Cover and refrigerate for 2 hours, or until firm enough to cut into rounds.
- Using a 7-cm (3-in) biscuit cutter, cut out chicken-and-mushroom patties.
- Coat croquettes thoroughly with breadcrumbs, followed by egg mixture. Coat again with breadcrumbs.
- Heat oil for deep-frying. Fry croquettes until golden brown and drain well. Serve immediately with chilli sauce, if desired.

macaroni with cheese and mushrooms

A classic comfort food, this creamy dish is very soothing for the soul.
Serves 8

Ingredients

Elbow macaroni	1 kg (2 lb 3 oz)
Butter	4 Tbsp
White button mushrooms	300 g (10½ oz), caps wiped and chopped
Onion	1, peeled and finely chopped
Plain (all-purpose) flour	1 Tbsp
Dry mustard	¾ tsp
Salt	½ tsp
Ground black pepper	¼ tsp
Milk	375 ml (12 fl oz / 1½ cups)
Ham	8 slices, chopped
Grated Cheddar cheese	650 g (1 lb 10 oz)
Frozen peas	50 g (2 oz), defrosted
Chopped fresh parsley	280 g (10 oz), chopped (reserve some for garnish)
Fresh white breadcrumbs	250 g (12 oz)

Method

- Preheat oven to 200°C (400°F).

- Butter individual ramekins and set aside.

- Cook pasta in a large pot of boiling salted water until tender but still firm to the bite, stirring occasionally. Drain and set aside.

- Melt 2 Tbsp butter in a large pot over medium-high heat. Add mushrooms and onion and sauté until onion turns translucent.

- Stir in flour, mustard, salt, and pepper then cook for 1 minute. Gradually whisk in milk. Cook until sauce is smooth and slightly thickened, whisking constantly, for about 3 minutes. Remove from heat.

- Add ham, cheese, peas and parsley. Stir until cheese melts. Mix in pasta.

- Melt remaining butter in a small saucepan over medium heat. Add breadcrumbs and sauté until beginning to brown, about 3 minutes. Sprinkle breadcrumbs over pasta.

- Divide into ramekins and bake until pasta is heated through and golden brown, for about 20 minutes. Garnish as desired

MEAT & POULTRY

five-spice pork, mushroom and almond stir-fry

This dish is very colourful with the use of red capsicums and green asparagus.

Serves 4

Ingredients

Pork fillet	500 g (1 lb 1½ oz), trimmed and thinly sliced
Light soy sauce	2 Tbsp
Five-spice powder	3 tsp
Whole almonds (skins on)	60 g (2 oz)
Cooking oil	1½ Tbsp
Red onion	1, peeled and cut into thin wedges
Red capsicum (bell pepper)	1, seeded, cut into thin slices
Chinese flowering cabbage (*choy sum*)	1 bunch, separated and stems chopped
Asparagus	6 stalks, trimmed and cut into thirds
Shiitake mushrooms	200 g (7 oz), caps wiped and sliced
Oyster sauce	1 Tbsp
Bean sprouts	200 g (7 oz), tailed

Method

- In a mixing bowl, combine pork, soy sauce and five-spice powder. Set aside in the refrigerator to marinate for 30 minutes.
- Heat a wok over high heat. When near smoking, add almonds and stir-fry for 2 minutes or until toasted. Transfer onto a plate and set aside.
- In the same wok, heat 1 tsp oil. Add pork fillet. Stir-fry for 2 minutes or until browned. Transfer to plate.
- Add remaining oil to wok. Heat and add onion. Stir-fry for 1 minute. Add capsicum, cabbage stems, asparagus and mushrooms. Stir-fry for 30 seconds.
- Add oyster sauce and 1 tsp water. Cover and cook for 30 seconds. Remove cover.
- Return pork to wok with cabbage leaves. Stir-fry for 1–2 minutes or until heated through.
- Add almonds and bean sprouts. Stir-fry for another 30 seconds. Transfer to a serving dish and serve hot.

NOTE

For a variation to the recipe, replace almonds with peanuts, cashews or macadamia nuts.

chinese chicken and mushroom parcels

These steamed Chinese chicken mushroom parcels make a healthy and refreshing dish.

Serves 4

Ingredients

Salt	1 Tbsp
Water	2 litres (64 fl oz / 8 cups)
Chinese cabbage	1 head, small, leaves separated
Garlic	1 clove, peeled
Ginger	2-cm (1-in) knob, peeled
Spring onions (scallions)	2, roughly chopped
Coriander leaves (cilantro)	2 sprigs, roughly chopped
Red chilli	1
Thai fish sauce	1 Tbsp
Chicken thighs	2, skin removed and roughly chopped
Dried Chinese mushrooms	4, soaked to soften, stems discarded and sliced
Lime	1, squeezed for juice and grated for zest
Cooking oil	1 tsp
Roasted white sesame seeds	1 Tbsp

Method

- Add salt to water and bring to the boil. Blanch cabbage leaves for 2 minutes to soften. Remove and plunge into ice water then drain and set aside.
- Using a food processor, process garlic, ginger, spring onions, coriander, chilli and fish sauce with a pinch of salt. Add chicken, mushrooms, lime juice and zest and process until mixture has the consistency of minced meat.
- Spoon 1 Tbsp minced mixture about 2-cm (1-in) from stem end of each cabbage leaf. Roll up to form neat parcels.
- Oil a steaming plate and place cabbage parcels on plate. Arrange parcels close to one another to prevent them from unravelling. Steam for about 7 minutes until cooked.
- Remove from steamer. Sprinkle sesame seeds on top and serve with sweet chilli sauce if desired.

vegetables & salads

portobello burger **84**

mushroom curry with potatoes **87**

braised trio of mushrooms **88**

twice-baked potatoes with mushrooms **91**

potato and portobello gratin **92**

pizza funghi **95**

insalata di funghi **96**

asian noodle, mushroom and cabbage salad **99**

quiche aux champignons **100**

spinach and mushroom pies **103**

bean curd with japanese mushroom sauce **104**

portobello burger

The portobello mushroom is large and has a meaty texture, making it ideal as a pattie for a vegetarian burger.

Serves 4

Ingredients

Olive oil	2 Tbsp
Garlic	1 clove, peeled and chopped
Balsamic vinegar	2 Tbsp
Thyme	2 sprigs
Portobello mushrooms	4, caps wiped
Salt	to taste
Ground black pepper	to taste
Burger buns	4, split and toasted
Lettuce leaves	8
Tomato	1, sliced
Mustard (optional)	

Caramelised Onions

Butter	50 g (2 oz)
Sugar	1 tsp
Onions	3, peeled and thinly sliced
Salt	to taste
Ground black pepper	to taste

Method

- Prepare caramelised onions. Heat butter in a medium-sized pan over medium heat. Add sugar and onions then season with salt and pepper. Cook until onions have caramelised, stirring occasionally to prevent onions from burning, for 10–15 minutes. Remove from pan and set aside.
- Preheat grill to medium-high heat.
- Whisk olive oil, garlic and balsamic vinegar in bowl. Strip leaves from sprigs of thyme and add to bowl. Brush mushroom caps all over with flavoured olive oil.
- Grill mushrooms, turning as needed, until tender but not mushy for about 6–8 minutes per side. Season with salt and pepper.
- Spread some mustard on the bottom half of each burger bun, if desired, then top with lettuce, tomato slices, a portobello mushroom and caramelised onions before covering with top half of bun. Serve immediately.

mushroom curry with potatoes

This mild curry is not fiery hot, but has enough spice to make it a flavourful curry to enjoy with a bowl of white rice.

Serves 4

Ingredients

Cooking oil	2 Tbsp
Mustard seeds	1 tsp
Cumin seeds	1 tsp
Ground coriander	1 tsp
Curry leaves	a handful
Ginger	2-cm (1-in) knob, peeled and grated
Onion	1, peeled and chopped
Garlic	2 cloves, peeled and chopped
Chilli powder	1 tsp
Ground turmeric	1 tsp
Tomato	1 kg (2 lb 3 oz), blended
Water	150 ml (5 fl oz / $^2/_3$ cup)
Coconut milk	200 ml (6$^1/_2$ fl oz / $^5/_6$ cup)
White button mushrooms	300 g (10$^1/_2$ oz), caps wiped and halved
Potatoes	200 g (7 oz), peeled and diced
Salt	to taste

Method

- Heat oil in a pan. When hot, add mustard seeds. When mustard seeds pop, add cumin seeds, ground coriander, curry leaves and ginger. Stir-fry for a few minutes.
- Add onion and garlic. Sauté until brown and onion turns soft. Add chilli powder and turmeric and stir for another minute.
- Add tomatoes and cook for a few minutes then stir in water and coconut milk.
- Bring to the boil then stir in mushrooms and diced potatoes. Season with salt to taste.
- Cover and simmer, stirring occasionally, until potatoes are tender. Remove and serve hot.

braised trio of mushrooms

This easy-to-prepare dish uses three different types of mushrooms for texture and is flavoured with garlic, oyster sauce and Chinese cooking wine.

Serves 4

Ingredients

Cooking oil	1 Tbsp
Chopped garlic	2 tsp
Dried Chinese mushrooms	5, soaked to soften, stems discarded and quartered
Straw mushrooms	225 g (7½ oz), washed and trimmed
Canned button mushrooms	75 g (2½ oz), washed and sliced
Spring onions (scallions)	2, finely chopped

Sauce

Light soy sauce	1 Tbsp
Chinese cooking wine (*hua tiao*)	2 Tbsp
Oyster sauce	3 Tbsp
Sugar	2 tsp
Chicken stock	60 ml (2 fl oz / ¼ cup)

Method

- Prepare sauce. Combine soy sauce, wine, oyster sauce, sugar and chicken stock. Set aside.
- Heat oil in a wok. Add garlic and lightly fry for 1 minute.
- Add all mushrooms and stir-fry, mixing well for a few seconds.
- Pour in sauce and lower heat. Cook for about 7 minutes, stirring continually until mushrooms are thoroughly cooked.
- Mix in spring onions, stirring for a few seconds. Transfer to a bowl and serve immediately.

twice-baked potatoes with mushrooms

These mushroom-embellished baked potatoes can be enjoyed on their own or served as side dishes.

Serves 4

Ingredients

Potatoes	4, large
Olive oil	for brushing
Swiss brown mushrooms	200 g (7 oz), caps wiped and sliced
Shallots	2, peeled and finely sliced
Fresh thyme leaves	1 tsp
Grated Parmesan cheese	250 g (9 oz)
Cream cheese	250 g (9 oz)
Egg yolk	1
Salt	to taste
Ground black pepper	to taste

Method

- Preheat oven to 200°C (400°F).
- Prick potatoes all over and brush with olive oil. Bake for 1 hour or until tender.
- Heat 1 Tbsp oil in a pan over moderate heat. Add mushrooms and shallots and cook until mushrooms are tender. Remove from heat. Stir in thyme leaves.
- Slice the tops off potatoes lengthways. Carefully scoop flesh into a mixing bowl, leaving skins intact. Add cheeses and egg yolk to potato flesh and mash. Lightly fold in mushrooms. Season with salt and pepper to taste.
- Spoon mixture back into potato skins, pressing down so skins are well-packed. Sprinkle with Parmesan cheese over and bake for 5–8 minutes or until heated through. Serve hot.

potato and portobello gratin

This oven-baked delicious mushroom- and- potato dish is a no-fuss crowd pleaser.

Serves 4

Ingredients

Portobello mushrooms	700 g (1½ lb)
Olive oil	4 Tbsp
Garlic	4 cloves, peeled and minced
Potatoes	2 kg (4 lb 6 oz) peeled and cut into 0.5-cm (¼-in) thick slices
Chopped fresh parsley	50 g (2 oz)
Salt	2 tsp
Ground black pepper	1 tsp
Grated Parmesan cheese	2 Tbsp
Light (single) cream	85 ml (2½ fl oz / ⅓ cup)

Method

- Remove and chop stems of portobello mushrooms. Place in a large mixing bowl. Using a small spoon, scrape away dark gills from mushroom caps and discard. Cut caps into 1-cm (½-in) pieces and add to bowl.
- Heat olive oil in a large frying pan over medium-high heat. Add chopped mushrooms then sauté for 4 minutes. Stir in garlic and sauté until mushrooms are tender, for about 10 minutes. Season with salt and pepper. Remove from heat.
- Preheat oven to 200°C (400°F).
- Combine potatoes, parsley, salt and pepper in a large mixing bowl. Toss and mix well.
- Spoon one-quarter of potato mixture into a medium-sized greased baking dish. Spread one-third of mushroom mixture on top. Repeat layering, ending with a layer of potatoes on top.
- Pour cream over to cover potatoes then cover dish with aluminium foil.
- Bake for 45 minutes then remove foil and bake again until top is brown and potatoes are tender. This will take another 40 minutes. Serve hot.

pizza funghi

This crusty pizza is topped with tomatoes, cheese and mushrooms.
Serves 2

Ingredients

Olive oil	1 Tbsp + 1 tsp
Onion	1, small, peeled and finely chopped
White button mushrooms	110 g (4 oz), stems discarded, caps wiped and sliced
Canned peeled tomatoes	390 g (14 oz), drained and coarsely chopped
Instant pizza crust	1
Grated mozzarella cheese	175 g (6 oz)
Dried basil	1/2 tsp
Dried oregano	1/2 tsp
Salt	1/4 tsp
Ground black pepper	1/4 tsp

Method

- Preheat oven to 230°C (450°F).
- Grease a large baking tray with 1 tsp oil and set aside.
- Heat 1 Tbsp oil in a small frying pan over moderate heat. Add onion, stirring occasionally, for 5–7 minutes or until onion is soft and translucent but not brown.
- Add mushrooms and fry, stirring occasionally, for another 3 minutes or until tender. Remove pan from heat and set aside.
- Spread chopped tomatoes on pizza base to cover completely. Sprinkle grated mozzarella cheese over evenly and top with prepared mushrooms.
- Sprinkle with dried herbs, salt and pepper. Bake for 12–15 minutes until crust is slightly brown. Serve hot.

insalata di funghi

A delicious first course, this salad may be accompanied by hot crusty bread.

Serves 4

Ingredients

Olive oil	3 Tbsp
Lemon juice	1 Tbsp
Salt	¼ tsp
Ground black pepper	a pinch
White button mushrooms	220 g (8 oz), caps wiped and thinly sliced
Green peas	60 g (2 oz), boiled
Lettuce	1 head, outer leaves discarded, leaves separated and shredded

Method

- In a small bowl, combine oil, lemon juice, salt and pepper for dressing. Mix well and set aside.
- Place mushrooms and peas in a mixing bowl. Pour dressing over and toss well. Refrigerate for 30 minutes.
- Line a medium-sized serving dish with shredded lettuce. Remove mushroom and pea mixture from the refrigerator and spoon over salad leaves. Serve immediately.

asian noodle, mushroom and cabbage salad

A filling appetiser or light lunch meal, this should be served hot, straight from the stove.

Serves 4

Ingredients

Cooking oil	1 Tbsp
Chinese cabbage	700 g (1½ lb), thinly sliced
Ginger	2.5-cm (1-in) knob, peeled and minced
Garlic	2 cloves, peeled and minced
Dried Chinese mushrooms	12, soaked to soften, stems discarded and sliced
Light soy sauce	3 Tbsp
Egg noodles	500 g (17½ oz)
Sesame oil	85 ml (2½ fl oz / ⅓ cup)
Lemon juice	2 Tbsp
Rice vinegar	1 Tbsp
Sugar	2 tsp
Hard-boiled eggs	3; 2 thinly sliced, 1 chopped for garnish
Chopped coriander leaves (cilantro)	200 g (7 oz)
Roasted white sesame seeds	1 Tbsp
Salt	to taste
Ground black pepper	to taste
Spring onions (scallions)	2, chopped

Method

- Heat oil in a wok over medium-high heat. Add cabbage, ginger, garlic and mushrooms. Stir-fry until cabbage wilts, for about 2 minutes. Remove from heat. Stir in 1 Tbsp soy sauce. Mix well.
- Cook noodles in a large pot of boiling salted water until just tender but still firm to the bite. Drain well and set aside in a large bowl.
- To make dressing, combine sesame oil, lemon juice, rice vinegar, sugar and remaining soy sauce in small bowl. Add dressing to noodles.
- Add sliced eggs, coriander and cabbage mixture. Toss well and season with salt and pepper.
- Sprinkle chopped spring onions, chopped egg and toasted sesame seeds over. Serve immediately.

quiche aux champignons

A marvellously tasty dish, Quiche aux Champignons may be served either hot or cold.

Serves 6

Ingredients

Shortcrust Pastry

Plain (all-purpose) flour	175 g (6 oz)
Chilled unsalted butter	85 g (3 oz), cut into large cubes
Egg yolk	1
Water	2 Tbsp
Salt	1 tsp

Filling

Butter	55 g (2 oz)
Shallots	2, peeled and finely chopped
Swiss brown mushrooms	500 g (17$\frac{1}{2}$ oz), caps wiped and thinly sliced
Salt	$\frac{1}{4}$ tsp
Ground white pepper	$\frac{1}{4}$ tsp
Grated nutmeg	$\frac{1}{4}$ tsp
Light (single) cream	125 ml (4 fl oz / $\frac{1}{2}$ cup)
Eggs	3
Grated Cheddar cheese	55 g (2 oz)

Method

- Preheat oven to 200°C (400°F).
- Prepare shortcrust pastry. Rub butter into flour until mixture resembles breadcrumbs. Add egg yolk and water, mixing until a smooth dough is formed. Refrigerate for 30 minutes.
- Roll out pastry dough on a floured work surface until just large enough to line a 22.5-cm (9-in) flan tin. Press into tin and trim off any excess dough. Place a sheet of baking paper into tin and fill with baking beans. Bake for 8–10 minutes until crust is golden brown. Remove baking paper and baking beans. Set aside.
- Prepare filling. Melt butter in a large frying-pan over moderate heat. When foam subsides, add shallots and cook, stirring occasionally for 3–4 minutes or until soft and translucent but not brown.
- Add mushrooms to pan and cook, stirring occasionally for 3 minutes. Remove pan from heat and stir in salt, pepper and nutmeg. Set aside.
- Combine cream, eggs and grated cheese in a medium-sized mixing bowl and beat well to blend. Mix well with mushrooms.
- Pour mixture into flan tin. Place in the centre of oven and bake for 25–30 minutes or until filling is set and firm and golden brown on top.
- Remove from the oven and serve hot or at room temperature.

spinach and mushroom pies

These spinach and mushroom pies are made with light puff pastry that crumbles and melts in your mouth with every bite.

Serves 4

Ingredients

Olive oil	1 Tbsp
Shallots	3, peeled and sliced
Garlic	3 cloves, peeled and chopped
Spinach	1 bunch, stalks and leaves separated and chopped
Oyster mushrooms	10, caps wiped and sliced
White button mushrooms	10, caps wiped and sliced
Ground cumin	1 tsp
Ground coriander	1 tsp
Lemon	1, squeezed for juice
Salt	to taste
Ground black pepper	to taste
Frozen puff pastry	500 g (17$\frac{1}{2}$ oz)
Egg yolk	1, lightly beaten

Method

- Preheat oven to 200°C (400°F). Prepare 4 pie dishes, each about 10-cm (4-in) in diameter.
- Heat olive oil in a saucepan over low heat. Add shallots and garlic and sauté until shallots turn translucent.
- Add spinach stalks and sauté for 3 minutes. Add mushrooms and cook until softened. Season with ground cumin and coriander then drizzle in 1 Tbsp lemon juice.
- Add spinach leaves and remaining lemon juice. Season with salt and pepper. Cook for about 2 minutes until spinach leaves wilt then remove from heat. Strain and set aside. Save strained liquid for later use.
- Roll out puff pastry thinly. Using a 10-cm (4-in) round pastry cutter, cut out 4 rounds to use as pie tops. Using a 12.5-cm (5-in) round pastry cutter, cut out another 4 rounds to use as pie bases.
- Press larger rounds of puff pastry into pie dishes. Spoon one-quarter of spinach mixture and 1–2 Tbsp strained liquid into each dish. Cover with smaller rounds of puff pastry then press edges down firmly to seal.
- Brush pie tops with beaten egg yolk and bake for 25–30 minutes or until puff pastry is golden brown. Serve immediately.

bean curd with japanese mushroom sauce

This savoury Japanese mushroom sauce goes well with the bland flavour of bean curd.

Serves 4

Ingredients

Firm bean curd	4 pieces
Olive oil	4 Tbsp
Garlic	2 cloves, peeled and chopped
Shiitake mushrooms	250 g (9 oz), stems discarded, caps wiped and sliced
Enokitake mushrooms	250 g (9 oz), trimmed and separated into small bunches
White button mushrooms	250 g (9 oz), stems discarded, caps wiped and sliced
Sake	2 Tbsp
Light soy sauce	$1\frac{1}{2}$ Tbsp
Dashi	150 ml (5 fl oz / $\frac{2}{3}$ cup)
Spring onions (scallions)	2, chopped
Corn flour (cornstarch)	2 tsp, mixed with 2 Tbsp water

Method

- Line a plate with absorbent paper. Place bean curd on it and cover with another layer of absorbent paper. Place a plate on top and set aside for 10 minutes. This is to drain excess water from bean curd. Pat bean curd dry and sprinkle some salt over to achieve a crisp crust when fried.
- Heat oil in a pan over medium-high heat. Fry both sides of bean curd until golden brown. Drain well on absorbent paper towels and transfer to serving plates. Reserve 2 Tbsp oil.
- In the same pan, reheat reserved oil. Sauté garlic and mushrooms over medium heat.
- Add sake, soy sauce and dashi then bring to the boil.
- Add spring onions and stir in corn flour mixture to thicken sauce. Remove from heat. Spoon over bean curd and serve immediately.

seafood

creamy salmon and mushroom pie **108**

mushrooms stuffed with tuna **111**

prawn, mushroom and asparagus stir-fry **112**

baked fish with mushrooms **115**

prawn and mushroom green curry **116**

shiitake and sake kamameishi **119**

stuffed squids with shiitake mushroom sauce **120**

creamy salmon and mushroom pie

Creamy and delicious, this fish pie makes a filling one-dish meal.
Serves 6–8

Ingredients

Salmon fillet	700 g (1½ lb), skinned and diced
Salt	to taste
Ground black pepper	to taste
Milk	600 ml (20 fl oz / 2½ cups)
Swiss brown mushrooms	225 g (7½ oz), caps wiped, trimmed and quartered
Potatoes	900 g (2 lb), peeled and quartered
Butter	25 g (1 oz)
Grated nutmeg	a dash

Sauce

Unsalted butter	50 g (2 oz)
Onion	1, peeled and chopped
Celery	½ stalk, chopped
Plain (all-purpose) flour	50 g (2 oz)
Lemon juice	10 ml (⅓ fl oz / 2 tsp)
Fresh parsley	2 sprigs, chopped
Salt	to taste
Ground black pepper	to taste

Method

- Preheat oven to 200°C (400°F).
- Season salmon with salt and pepper. In a pot, bring milk to the boil then remove from heat. Add mushrooms and salmon, cover the pot and let it gently poach for 20 minutes.
- Using a slotted spoon, transfer salmon and mushrooms to a 1.5 litre (48 fl oz / 6 cups) baking dish or into individual ramekins. Reserve poaching liquid and set aside.
- Immerse potatoes in cold water in a pot. Add a pinch of salt and boil for 20 minutes. Drain and mash with butter and milk. Season with salt, pepper and nutmeg to taste and set aside.
- Prepare sauce. Melt butter in a pan. Add onion and celery and sauté until onion is translucent.
- Stir in flour and remove from heat. Slowly add reserved poaching liquid, stirring until a sauce is formed. Return pan to heat. Stir and simmer to thicken.
- Add lemon juice and parsley. Season with salt and pepper then add to baking dish or ramekins.
- Top with mashed potatoes and bake in the oven for 30–40 minutes until golden brown. Serve hot.

mushrooms stuffed with tuna

For a light lunch, serve the mushrooms on toast with a simple watercress and tomato salad on the side.

Serves 4

Ingredients

Large white button mushrooms	8, stems minced and caps left whole
Butter	50 g (2 oz)
Water	8 tsp
Onion	1, small, peeled and finely chopped
Canned tuna	200 g (7 oz), drained and flaked
Fresh white breadcrumbs	25 g (1 oz)
Salt	to taste
Ground black pepper	to taste
Herb and garlic flavoured cheese	75 g (3 oz)

Method

- Heat a grill to moderate heat.
- Place mushroom caps, with the underside facing up, on grill rack. Use half the butter to dot the centres of mushrooms and sprinkle each one with 1 tsp water. Sprinkling water on the mushrooms helps keep them moist. Grill for 10 minutes, until just tender.
- Meanwhile, melt remaining butter in a pan. Add onion and minced mushroom stems. Fry gently for 5 minutes until onion is soft.
- Remove pan from heat and add tuna and breadcrumbs. Mix well and season to taste with salt and pepper.
- Spoon some tuna mixture into mushroom caps and top with some cheese. Grill mushrooms for another 3–4 minutes, until cheese is golden and beginning to melt. Serve at once.

SEAFOOD

prawn, mushroom and asparagus stir-fry

A quick stir-fry of crunchy asparagus, prawns and juicy mushrooms.
Serves 4

Ingredients

Light soy sauce	90 ml (3 fl oz / ³⁄₈ cup)
Honey	2 Tbsp
Prawns (shrimps)	600 g (1 lb 5 oz), peeled and deveined
White button mushrooms	300 g (11 oz), stems discarded, caps wiped and thickly sliced
Cooking oil	2 Tbsp
Red onion	1, small, peeled and cut into wedges
Chinese flowering cabbage (*choy sum*)	1 bunch, leaves and stems separated and chopped
Asparagus	6 stalks, trimmed and cut into 5-cm (2-in) lengths

Method

- Mix light soy sauce and honey together to form a marinade.
- Place prawns and mushrooms into separate bowls. Pour half the marinade over prawns and remaining half over mushrooms. Mix well then cover and refrigerate for 15 minutes.
- Heat 1 Tbsp oil in a wok over high heat. Add prawns and stir-fry for 1–2 minutes or until pink. Transfer to a plate and set aside.
- Add remaining oil and onion to wok. Stir-fry for 1 minute. Add cabbage stems and asparagus. Stir-fry for another minute.
- Add marinated mushrooms and stir-fry for 2 minutes or until mushrooms are almost tender.
- Add prawns and cabbage leaves. Stir-fry for 1 minute or until leaves just wilt. Transfer to a serving dish and serve hot.

baked fish with mushrooms

A great way to enjoy baked fish. The breadcrumbs create a golden brown crust that breaks away to expose the succulent fish and mushrooms beneath.

Serves 4

Ingredients

Olive oil	3 Tbsp
Shiitake mushrooms	200 g (7 oz), stems discarded, caps wiped and thinly sliced
White button mushrooms	200 g (7 oz), caps wiped and thinly sliced
Dried breadcrumbs	750 g (1 lb 5 oz)
Grated Parmesan cheese	50 g (2 oz)
Fresh parsley	1 bunch, chopped
White fish fillet	4, skinless, each about 160 g
Salt	a pinch
Ground black pepper	1/4 tsp
Sour cream	60 ml (2 fl oz / 1/4 cup)
Japanese mayonnaise	3 Tbsp

Method

- Preheat oven to 200°C (400°F).
- Heat 2 Tbsp oil over medium heat in a large pan. Add shiitake and button mushrooms and sauté for 5–7 minutes or until tender. Transfer to a large bowl.
- In a separate frying pan, heat remaining oil over medium heat. Add breadcrumbs and cook for 3 minutes or until lightly toasted. Add to bowl of mushrooms then toss with cheese and parsley.
- Place fish in a single layer in a baking dish. Sprinkle salt and pepper over.
- In a small bowl, stir together sour cream and mayonnaise. Spread mixture over fish then spoon mushroom mixture over. Bake for 25 minutes or until fish flakes when pressed with a fork and is cooked through. Serve hot.

prawn and mushroom green curry

This Thai green curry is a refreshing change from the usual red curries.
Serves 2

Ingredients

Cooking oil	1 Tbsp
Ginger	1-cm (½-in) knob, peeled and grated
Garlic	1 clove, peeled and crushed
Tiger prawns (shrimps)	225 g (7½ oz), peeled and deveined, leaving tail intact
Straw mushrooms	350 g (12 oz), halved
Thai green curry paste	1 Tbsp
Thai fish sauce	1 tsp
Sugar	a pinch
Coconut milk	250 ml (8 fl oz / 1 cup)

Method

- Heat oil in a wok. Add ginger, garlic and prawns. Stir-fry for 2 minutes or until prawns change colour.
- Add 1 Tbsp water to prevent prawns from sticking to wok. Add mushrooms and fry for another minute.
- Add remaining ingredients to wok and simmer for 2 minutes. Ladle into a serving bowl and serve hot with rice.

shiitake and sake kamameishi

Kamameshi is a popular Japanese rice dish that is prepared in one pot.
Serves 4

Ingredients

Short-grain rice	350 g (12 oz), washed and drained
Shiitake mushrooms	3, soaked to soften, stems discarded and sliced
Salmon fillet	200 g (7 oz)
Enokitake mushrooms	1 bundle, 200 g (7 oz) trimmed
Carrot	55g (2 oz), diced
Edamame	55g (2 oz), pods removed
Water	375 ml (12 fl oz / 1½ cups)
Dashi	375 ml (12 fl oz / 1½ cups)
Sake	2 Tbsp
Light soy sauce	1½ Tbsp
Salt	½ tsp
Roasted white sesame seeds	1 tsp

Method

- Combine all ingredients except sesame seeds in a large pot and mix well.
- Cover and cook over a low-moderate heat until rice is cooked and fluffy. This will take 20–30 minutes.
- Flake salmon and mix with rice.
- Garnish with sesame seeds and serve hot.

stuffed squids with shiitake mushroom sauce

These squids are stuffed with ground pork and served with a savoury mushroom sauce.

Serves 4

Ingredients

Minced pork	225 g (7½ oz)
Chopped coriander leaves (cilantro)	1 tsp
Ground white pepper	¼ tsp
Minced garlic	1 Tbsp
Thai fish sauce	1 tsp
Sugar	1 tsp
Light soy sauce	1 Tbsp
Egg	1, lightly beaten
Finely chopped onion	1 tsp
Squids	6–8, cleaned and left whole

Mushroom Sauce

Cooking oil	60 ml (2 fl oz / ¼ cup)
Minced garlic	1 tsp
Ginger	2.5-cm (1-in) knob, peeled and shredded
Dried Chinese mushrooms	6–8, stems discarded, soaked to soften and sliced
Oyster sauce	1 Tbsp
Water	1 Tbsp
Spring onions (scallions)	3, cut into 2.5-cm (1-in) lengths

Method

- In a bowl, mix together pork, coriander, pepper, garlic, fish sauce, sugar, soy sauce, egg and onion. Mix well to bind. Using a small spoon or your hands, carefully stuff pork mixture into squids.
- Place squids into a steamer and steam for 10–15 minutes. Remove and cut into 2-cm (1-in) slices. Transfer onto a serving plate. Cover to keep warm and set aside.
- Prepare sauce. Heat oil in a wok, add garlic and ginger and fry over medium heat for 30 seconds until mixture is fragrant and garlic is slightly brown.
- Add mushrooms, oyster sauce and water then stir for 4–5 minutes until sauce is hot and bubbly.
- Stir in spring onions. Spoon sauce over squid slices and serve immediately.

rice & noodles

khumbi pullao (mushroom rice) **124**

mushroom and cashew chow mein **127**

udon with assorted mushrooms **128**

mixed mushroom lasagna **131**

egg noodles with mushrooms and bamboo shoots **132**

yaki udon with mushrooms **135**

fettuccine with shiitake mushroom sauce **136**

creamy garlic pasta with mushrooms **139**

khumbi pullao (mushroom rice)

This mushroom rice dish is popular in India and is enjoyed for its mildness and simplicity.

Serves 4

Ingredients

Basmati rice	375 g (12½ oz)
Butter	100 g (3½ oz)
White button mushrooms	350 g (12 oz), caps wiped and sliced
Onion	1, large, peeled and thinly sliced
Garlic	3 cloves, peeled and finely chopped
Cloves	5
Cardamoms	5
Cinnamon	1 stick, about 10-cm (4-in) in length
Bay leaf	1
Cumin seeds	2 tsp
Aniseed	1 tsp
Salt	to taste
Ground black pepper	to taste
Boiling water	575 ml, (18½ fl oz / 2⅓ cups)

Method

- Wash rice under cold running water and put into a large bowl. Cover with cold water for 30 minutes then drain and set aside.
- Heat butter in a large saucepan, add mushrooms and cook for 1–2 minutes over medium-heat, stirring constantly. Remove and keep warm.
- Add onion and garlic to the same pan and cook gently for 5–7 minutes until soft. Stir in spices, salt and pepper and cook for another minute.
- Add rice to pan. Stir for 1 minute and pour in boiling water. Bring to the boil then lower heat, cover and simmer for 15 minutes until rice is tender.
- Remove and discard spices if desired. Add half a portion of mushrooms to rice and mix well.
- Transfer to a serving dish and serve hot with remaining mushrooms.

mushroom and cashew chow mein

A simple Chinese noodle dish that can be served as part of a Chinese meal.

Serves 2

Ingredients

Sesame oil	1 Tbsp
Garlic	1 clove, peeled and chopped
Dried Chinese mushrooms	100 g (3½ oz), soaked to soften, stems discarded, halved or quartered
Baby corn	100 g (3½ oz), halved or quartered
Sugar peas	100 g (3½ oz)
Red chilli	1, seeds removed and sliced
Spring onions (scallions)	4–6, thinly sliced
Bean sprouts	30 g (1 oz)
Cashew nuts	10
Fresh egg noodles	250 g (9 oz), blanched
Dark soy sauce	1 Tbsp
Light brown sugar	½ Tbsp
Chinese cooking wine (*hua tiao*)	1 Tbsp
Oyster sauce	1 Tbsp

Method

- Heat oil in a wok until almost smoking then add garlic, mushrooms, baby corn, sugar peas and red chilli.
- Stir-fry for about 2 minutes then add spring onions, bean sprouts, cashew nuts and noodles. Mix well and fry for another 30 seconds.
- Season with soy sauce, sugar, wine and oyster sauce. Stir-fry for about 1 minute until noodles are heated through. Transfer to a serving dish and serve immediately.

udon with assorted mushrooms

Udon noodles with shiitake and enokitake mushrooms, carrots and firm bean curd in a miso broth.

Serves 4

Ingredients

Boiling water	1.5 litre (32 fl oz / 6 cups),
Instant white miso	6 x 8 g sachets
Udon	400 g (13½ oz)
Firm bean curd	300 g (10 oz), cut into cubes
Spring onions (scallions)	4, stalks ends trimmed, cut into 5-cm (2-in) lengths
Carrot	1, cut into thin sticks
Shiitake mushrooms	100 g (3½ oz), stems discarded and thinly sliced
Enokitake mushrooms	100 g (3½ oz), stems trimmed
Nori (seaweed)	1 sheet, thinly shredded

Method

- Combine water and miso in a large saucepan then bring to the boil over high heat. Reduce heat to low and add udon. Cook, stirring occasionally, for 3 minutes or until udon is heated through.

- Add bean curd, spring onions, carrot, mushrooms and three-quarters of the nori. Cook, stirring for 2 minutes or until heated through and well-combined.

- Ladle udon and soup into serving bowls. Sprinkle with remaining nori and serve immediately.

mixed-mushroom lasagna

This hearty tomato and mushroom lasagna makes a perfect vegetarian meal.

Serves 8

Ingredients

Olive oil	2 tsp
Minced garlic	1½ Tbsp
Dried oregano	2½ tsp
Canned chopped tomatoes	1 can
White wine	85 ml (2½ fl oz / ⅓ cup)
Salt	to taste
Ground black pepper	to taste
Swiss brown mushrooms	350 g (12 oz), caps wiped and sliced
White button mushrooms	350 g (12 oz), caps wiped and sliced
Lasagna sheets	12
Grated Parmesan cheese	55g (2 oz)

Method

- Preheat oven to 220°C (440°F).
- Heat ½ tsp oil in a large non-stick pan over medium-high heat. Add garlic and oregano then stir for 30 seconds.
- Add chopped tomatoes and wine then bring to the boil. Reduce heat and simmer until slightly thickened, for about 6 minutes. Season with salt and pepper then set tomato sauce aside.
- Heat ½ tsp oil in another large non-stick pan over medium-high heat. Add mushrooms and sauté until mushrooms begin to release juices, about 9 minutes. Season with salt and pepper. Set aside.
- Spread one-third of tomato sauce over the bottom of a greased lasagna dish and lay 3 lasagna sheets crosswise over. Sprinkle one-quarter of Parmesan cheese on top then spoon one-third of mushrooms over. Repeat layering twice then top dish with remaining sheets of lasagna and sprinkle remaining Parmesan cheese over.
- Cover lasagna with foil and bake for 20 minutes. Remove foil and continue baking until pasta sheets are tender and top is golden, about 25 minutes. Let stand for 10 minutes. Serve hot.

egg noodles with mushrooms and bamboo shoots

This easy-to-make dish may be served as part of a Chinese meal or on its own.

Serves 4

Ingredients

Cooking oil	4 Tbsp
Garlic	1 clove, peeled and chopped
Canned bamboo shoots	375 g (12½ oz), drained and thinly sliced
Dried Chinese mushrooms	12, soaked to soften, stems discarded and halved if large
Chinese cooking wine (*hua tiao*)	2 Tbsp
Light soy sauce	4 Tbsp
Sugar	1 Tbsp
Water	90 ml (3 fl oz / 6 Tbsp)
Spring onions (scallions)	2, chopped
Fresh egg noodles	250 g (9 oz), blanched

Method

- Heat a heavy-based frying pan over high heat for 30 seconds. Add oil and swirl around pan. Add garlic and fry for a minute.
- Add bamboo shoots and mushrooms. Stir-fry for 5 minutes.
- Add wine, soy sauce, sugar and water. Cover pan and simmer over low heat for 10 minutes.
- Remove cover and add spring onions and noodles. Cook for another 1 minute and mix well. Transfer to a serving dish and serve hot.

yaki udon with mushrooms

This is a hearty dish of stir-fried udon with carrot, mushrooms, red capsicum and cabbage.

Serves 2

Ingredients

Udon	100 g (3½ oz)
Cooking oil	2 Tbsp
Carrot	1, cut into thin sticks
Onion	½, peeled and diced
Shiitake mushrooms	100 g (3½ oz), stems discarded and sliced
Red capsicum (bell pepper)	1, seeded and sliced
Garlic	1 clove, peeled and chopped
Cabbage	½, sliced
Spring onions (scallions)	2, finely sliced

Sauce

Oyster sauce	2 Tbsp
Chinese cooking wine (*hua tiao*)	1 Tbsp
Sugar	1 tsp
Light soy sauce	1 tsp
Sesame oil	½ tsp

Method

- In a small bowl, mix sauce ingredients together and set aside.
- Cook udon noodles according to instructions on pack. Drain and rinse under cold water to remove excess starch and set aside.
- Heat oil in a wok. Add carrot and onion and stir-fry until onion turns translucent.
- Add mushrooms, capsicum, garlic and cabbage, then stir-fry until cabbage is soft.
- Add udon and sauce mixture. Stir fry until udon is well-coated with sauce.
- Garnish with spring onions and serve hot.

RICE & NOODLES

fettuccine with shiitake mushroom sauce

Fettuccine bathed in an aromatic and velvety shiitake mushroom sauce.

Serves 2

Ingredients

Dried Chinese mushrooms	30 g (1 oz)
Olive oil	1 Tbsp
Bacon	6 slices, minced
Shallots	3, peeled and minced
White button mushrooms	110 g (4 oz), caps wiped and sliced
Dried rosemary	1/2 tsp
Beef stock	250 ml (8 fl oz / 1 cup)
Light (single) cream	300 ml (10 fl oz / 1 1/4 cups)
Cooked fettuccine	200 g (7 oz)
Grated Parmesan cheese	140 g (5 oz)
Salt	to taste
Ground black pepper	to taste
Chopped parsley	1 tsp

Method

- Soak mushrooms in water for 30 minutes. Drain and reserve soaking liquid. Slice the mushrooms.

- Heat oil in a large frying pan over medium heat. Add bacon and cook until fat renders, stirring frequently for about 3 minutes. Pour away half the fat then add shallots and sauté for 1 minute.

- Add mushrooms and rosemary and sauté for another 3 minutes. Add stock and reserved liquid.

- Bring to the boil, lower heat and simmer for 10 minutes. Add cream and simmer for another 5 minutes. Remove from heat.

- Add pasta and mix well. Mix in Parmesan cheese. Season with salt and pepper to taste. Transfer to serving plates. Sprinkle with parsley and serve hot.

creamy garlic pasta with mushrooms

This delicious pasta dish may be served together with a fresh green salad to make a substantial dinner.

Serves 2

Ingredients

Chicken stock	250 ml (8 fl oz / 1 cup)
Whipping cream	180 ml (6 oz / ¾ cup)
Garlic	3 cloves, peeled and crushed
Dried chilli flakes	¼ tsp
Grated Parmesan cheese	110 g (4 oz)
Butter	1 Tbsp
White button mushrooms	12, caps wiped and cut into 1-cm (½-in) slices
Bacon	8 slices, cut crosswise into 1-cm (½-in) wide strips
Cooked penne	300 g (10 oz)
Frozen green peas	250 g (9 oz), defrosted

Method

- Mix stock, cream, garlic and chilli flakes in a medium saucepan. Bring to mixture the boil then reduce heat and simmer for 20 minutes. Remove from heat and stir in Parmesan cheese. Cover sauce to keep warm.

- Melt butter in a large non-stick pan over medium-high heat. Add mushrooms and sauté until brown, for about 7 minutes. Remove from heat.

- In a separate pan, fry bacon until crisp. Drain well and set aside.

- Return sauce to heat then add mushrooms and peas. Stir over low heat for about 3 minutes then remove from heat and mix in bacon strips and pasta. Cover and let stand 1 minute.

- Transfer to individual bowls. Garnish with strips of bacon if desired and serve hot.

glossary

1. Shiitake mushrooms
These mushrooms have a smoky flavour and can be used in stir-fries, salads and stews. Dried shiitake mushrooms are also known as dried Chinese mushrooms. They have a more intense flavour that they acquire through the drying process. These mushrooms need to be soaked in water for about 30 minutes before using. Squeeze out the excess water and use the soaking liquid to add more flavour to dishes.

2. Wood ear fungus
Although rather bland in taste, the wood ear fungus is valued for its crunchy texture. Soak the dried fungus in water for 30 minutes before use.

3. Oyster mushrooms
These mushrooms are identified by their fan shape and oyster flavour.

4. Portobello mushrooms (picture not shown)
Portobello mushrooms are in fact large cremini mushrooms. These meaty mushrooms can be grilled whole or sliced and sautéed. When cooked, these mushrooms sometimes produce a blackish liquid. To prevent this, scrape off the black gills before using.

5. Straw mushrooms
These small mushrooms have a distinct globe-like shape and are readily available in cans. They are commonly used in Chinese and Thai stir-fries and soups.

6. White button mushrooms
These mushrooms have round caps and short, thick stems. They can be eaten raw but are often cooked as this helps enhance their flavour. Most cooks simply wipe the caps clean before use, although some prefer to peel off the top layer from the caps.

7. Enokitake mushrooms (or Enoki mushrooms)
These long, thin-stemmed mushrooms originally grow wild but are today cultivated and easily available. Trim away the spongy root, then wash thoroughly. Enokitake mushrooms can be eaten cooked or raw.

8. Honshimeiji mushrooms
These mushrooms are mild in flavour but have a meaty texture similar to the oyster mushroom. They are commonly used in soups, grilled or fried. To use, cut off the hard base and brush off remaining dirt.

9. Swiss brown mushrooms
Swiss brown mushrooms are also commonly known as creminis. These mushrooms have a slightly stronger taste than the white button mushrooms and are commonly used in stews and pasta dishes.

10. Dashi
This is the basic stock for Japanese cooking. A basic dashi broth is made from kelp and bonito. Sachets of instant dashi powder are available in Asian supermarkets.

11. Miso paste
Miso is a paste made from fermenting soy beans with either rice, wheat or barley with yeast. Miso provides a deep salty flavour. It is used in many Japanese dishes.

12. Firm bean curd
Firm bean curd is pressed bean curd. It holds its shape when cooked and absorbs flavours better than soft bean curd.

13. Chinese cooking wine (*hua tiao*)
Made from fermented glutinous rice, Chinese cooking wine is today also commonly known as Shao Xing wine. Store in a cool, dark place, away from direct sunlight.

14. Transparent (glass) noodles
Transparent noodles have to be soaked in cold water for 20 minutes or in hot water for 3–5 minutes before use. It is commonly used in soups, stir-fries and spring rolls in Asian cuisine.

15. Vietnamese rice paper
These edible translucent sheets come in various shapes (round or square) and sizes (large or small). In their dried state, these thin wrappers are brittle. They need to be moistened with water before use.

16. Kaffir lime leaves
These leaves are from the kaffir lime plant and are recognised by their two distinct sections. They are frequently used in soups, stir-fries and curries.

17. Edamame
These are fresh soy beans, often sold still in their bright green pods. These short pods usually contain no more than three beans. Edamame is often served simply steamed and salted, then removed from the pods and eaten straight away.

18. Five-spice powder (picture not shown)
Cinnamon, Sichuan pepper, cloves, fennel seed and star anise are ground and combined to form this aromatic powder. This Chinese seasoning produces sweet, sour, salty, bitter and pungent flavours.

Weights and Measures

Quantities for this book are given in Metric, Imperial and American (spoon and cup) measures. Standard spoon and cup measurements used are: 1 tsp = 5 ml, 1 Tbsp = 15 ml, 1 cup = 250 ml. All measures are level unless stated.

Liquid And Volume Measures

Metric	Imperial	American
5 ml	⅙ fl oz	1 teaspoon
10 ml	⅓ fl oz	1 dessertspoon
15 ml	½ fl oz	1 tablespoon
60 ml	2 fl oz	¼ cup (4 tablespoons)
85 ml	2½ fl oz	⅓ cup
90 ml	3 fl oz	⅜ cup (6 tablespoons)
125 ml	4 fl oz	½ cup
180 ml	6 fl oz	¾ cup
250 ml	8 fl oz	1 cup
300 ml	10 fl oz (½ pint)	1¼ cups
375 ml	12 fl oz	1½ cups
435 ml	14 fl oz	1¾ cups
500 ml	16 fl oz	2 cups
625 ml	20 fl oz (1 pint)	2½ cups
750 ml	24 fl oz (1⅕ pints)	3 cups
1 litre	32 fl oz (1⅗ pints)	4 cups
1.25 litres	40 fl oz (2 pints)	5 cups
1.5 litres	48 fl oz (2⅖ pints)	6 cups
2.5 litres	80 fl oz (4 pints)	10 cups

Oven Temperature

	°C	°F	Gas Regulo
Very slow	120	250	1
Slow	150	300	2
Moderately slow	160	325	3
Moderate	180	350	4
Moderately hot	190/200	375/400	5/6
Hot	210/220	410/425	6/7
Very hot	230	450	8
Super hot	250/290	475/550	9/10

Dry Measures

Metric	Imperial
30 grams	1 ounce
45 grams	1½ ounces
55 grams	2 ounces
70 grams	2½ ounces
85 grams	3 ounces
100 grams	3½ ounces
110 grams	4 ounces
125 grams	4½ ounces
140 grams	5 ounces
280 grams	10 ounces
450 grams	16 ounces (1 pound)
500 grams	1 pound, 1½ ounces
700 grams	1½ pounds
800 grams	1¾ pounds
1 kilogram	2 pounds, 3 ounces
1.5 kilograms	3 pounds, 4½ ounces
2 kilograms	4 pounds, 6 ounces

Length

Metric	Imperial
0.5 cm	¼ inch
1 cm	½ inch
1.5 cm	¾ inch
2.5 cm	1 inch

Abbreviation

tsp	teaspoon
Tbsp	tablespoon
g	gram
kg	kilogram
ml	millilitre